Busy Little HANDS

Learning Activities for **PRESCHOOLERS**

SCIENCE PLAY!

Susan Edwards Richmond

Storey Publishing

WHAT DO YOU WONDER ABOUT?

Science is all about wondering— and then finding out.

Every time you . . .

| ASK a question | GUESS the answer | TRY it out | SEE what happens | and THINK about the results . . . |

YOU are being a scientist!

THIS BOOK IS FOR YOU, SCIENTIST.

EXPLORE YOUR WORLD!

How do objects move?

How do things look, feel, smell, sound, and taste?

How do things change?

How do plants and animals live and grow?

Start with any activity you like!

FAMILIES AND TEACHERS

The activities in this book introduce fundamental concepts from four fields of science—physics, earth science, chemistry, and biology. See pages 44–47 for more information about how children naturally practice the steps of the scientific method and how you can support their explorations. Don't forget to have fun!

PULLEY-UP

HOW HIGH CAN YOU LIFT A HEAVY LOAD?

GROWN-UP PREP STEPS

Gather a 6- to 10-foot length of rope and a bucket to make a pulley system. Help your child collect heavy objects, such as toys, filled water bottles, or rocks. Find a tree with low branches or a play set with horizontal bars. Extend the activity by changing the weight of the load and the height of the pulley.

1

Tie a long rope to the handle of a bucket. Put a few heavy objects in the bucket.

2

Try to lift the bucket by the handle or rope. How does it feel?

This is SO heavy!

4

3

Now loop the rope over a branch or bar to create a pulley system.

Wow, I can lift it above my head!

4

This time, pull down on the rope to lift the bucket.

Now how does it feel?

5

VINEGAR VOLCANO

BUILD A MOUNTAIN WITH A SECRET CENTER. WHAT HAPPENS WHEN YOU ADD VINEGAR?

1 tsp
5 mL

Dish Soap

Red Paint

8-Ounce Cup

Baking Soda

Vinegar

GROWN-UP PREP STEPS

Gather an 8-ounce plastic cup, about 4 ounces of water, 3 to 4 tablespoons of baking soda, 1 teaspoon of dish soap, a squeeze of red tempera paint, and 1 cup of white vinegar. Fill a plastic tub with sand, or do this activity outdoors in a sandbox.

1

Mound sand around the plastic cup to build your volcano!

2

Fill the cup halfway with water.

3

Mix the baking soda, dish soap, and paint into the water.

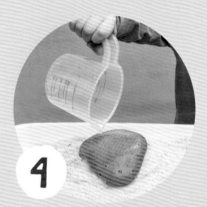

4

Slowly pour the vinegar into the cup. What happens?

Look at the lava bubbling over!

BLOOMING COLORS

HOW MANY COLORS ARE HIDDEN INSIDE ONE DOT?

GROWN-UP PREP STEPS

Gather several colors of washable markers, white coffee filters, a cup of water, and a dropper. Green, black, and brown markers will show the widest range of colors, but it's fun to experiment with them all!

1

Use a marker to color a dime-size dot in the center of a coffee filter.

2

Add one or two drops of water to your dot.

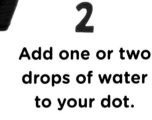

8

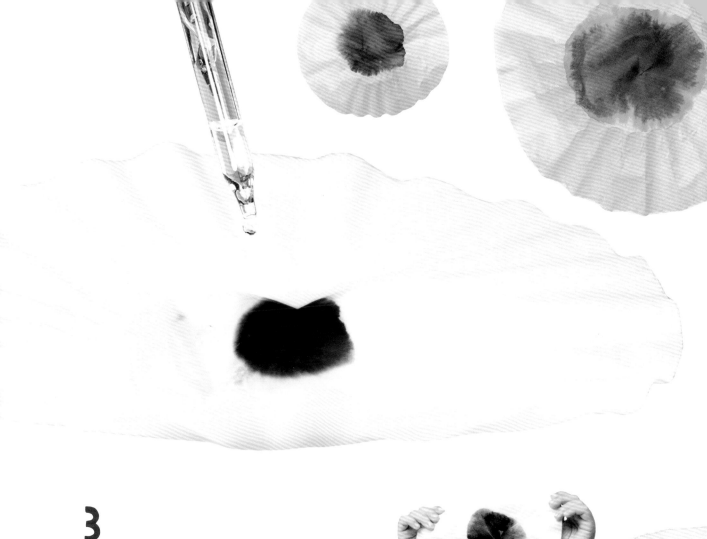

3

Watch the colors spread. What colors do you see?

4

Try using markers of different colors and making different kinds of marks. What do you see when the color spreads?

SEED START

WHAT DOES A SEED NEED TO GROW?

GROWN-UP PREP STEPS

Gather four 8-ounce paper cups, a small bag of potting soil, a small pitcher of water, and eight bean seeds. Any dry bean will work, but good choices include kidney, pinto, black, and navy beans. Extend the activity by comparing the seed's needs with the needs of other living things, including people!

Soil and Sunlight

Soil and Water

Here's what you will be giving the beans in each cup:

Soil, Water, and Sunlight

Water and Sunlight

Label your cups 1, 2, 3, and 4. Fill cups 1, 2, and 3 with a few inches of soil. Plant two beans in each, about 2 inches deep.

Place cup 1 in a sunny window, but do not water it.

10

Pour just enough water into cup 2 to moisten the soil.

Place the cup in a dark place.

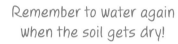

Remember to water again when the soil gets dry!

Pour just enough water into cup 3 to moisten the soil.

Place the cup in a sunny window.

Do not put soil in cup 4.

Put two beans in the cup and cover them with an inch of water.

Place the cup in a sunny window.

Check the cups daily for 1 to 2 weeks.

Which beans grew best? Why?

POLAR BEAR PAW

HOW DO ANIMALS STAY WARM IN FREEZING TEMPERATURES?

GROWN-UP PREP STEPS

Collect two 1-quart plastic ziplock bags, some vegetable shortening, and a silicone spatula. Fill a bowl with cold water and ice. Extend the activity by making another "paw" and filling it with other materials, such as wool, cotton, fur, or paper. Compare the results.

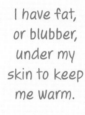

I have fat, or blubber, under my skin to keep me warm.

1

Turn one bag inside out and put it inside the other bag.

Use a spatula to fill the space between the two ziplock bags with shortening.

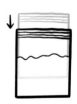

2

Zip the inner bag to the outer bag to seal in the shortening. Now you have a polar bear paw!

Brrrr!

3

Slip one hand into your insulated polar bear paw.

4

Put both hands in a bowl of ice water.

How does each hand feel?

13

RAIN, RAIN, COME TO STAY

HOW MUCH RAIN CAN YOU COLLECT IN YOUR RAIN JUG?

GROWN-UP PREP STEPS

Gather an empty plastic half-gallon milk jug or 1-liter bottle, scissors, a ruler, and a permanent marker. Extend the activity by encouraging your child to find a use for the water, such as watering houseplants.

1

Have a grown-up help you use scissors to cut off the tapered top of the jug or bottle.

4"

3"

2"

1"

2

Use a ruler to mark off your rain jug in inches or centimeters.

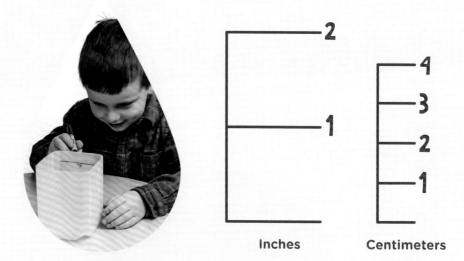

Inches   Centimeters

3

Place it out in the open before a rain shower.

4

Check it when the rain stops.

How much rain did it collect?

It rained more than an inch last night!

MYSTERY GOOP

SOLID, LIQUID, OR BOTH?

It's oozy!

GROWN-UP PREP STEPS

To make this goop that seems to shift back and forth between liquid and solid, all you need is a bowl, a cup of cornstarch, and half a cup of water.

Measure 1 cup of cornstarch into a big bowl. Add ½ cup of water.

Mix with your hands until goop forms.

It's pouring like a waterfall.

Let the mixture dribble from your fingers.

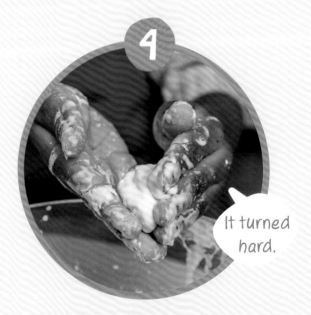

It turned hard.

Make a ball and toss it in the air. Experiment!

How does the mixture change?

BIODIVERSITY HOOP

HOW MANY LIVING THINGS CAN YOU FIND IN A SMALL SPACE?

GROWN-UP PREP STEPS

Find a lightweight hoop 30 to 40 inches in diameter (a loop of string or twine will work in a pinch). Get a pencil and paper to record findings. Extend the activity by counting at different times of day and under different weather conditions. Use field guides or an app such as iNaturalist to identify findings.

1

Place your hoop on the ground.

18

2

Count the number of different plants and bugs inside. Write down the number.

Why are there more bugs here?

There are three worms!

3

Lift the hoop and move it to different places. Count and record.

Where do you find the most living things?

KiTCHEN SiNK OR FLOAT

WHAT SINKS LIKE A STONE? WHAT FLOATS LIKE A BOAT?

GROWN-UP PREP STEPS

Help your child gather a variety of fruits and vegetables. Fill a tub or large bowl with water. To record results, create a chart like the one pictured below. Extend the activity by peeling or cutting up the foods to see if the results change.

	SINK	FLOAT	BOB
		✓	
			✓

1

Gather different fruits and vegetables from your kitchen.

The banana floats!

2

Place them in the water one at a time.

3

Which ones sink?

Which float?

Which bob just beneath the surface?

Mark the correct column on your chart!

Let's try the sweet potato!

SHADOW CLOCK

CAN YOU MAKE A SIMPLE CLOCK WITH JUST TWO STICKS?

GROWN-UP PREP STEPS

Start this activity in the morning! Find a spot outside that will get full sun. Help your child choose one straight stick to cast a shadow and another straight stick to represent the hour hand of a clock. A bowl filled with sand or gravel can hold the shadow stick in place. If the ground is soft enough, you can also push the stick directly into the soil.

2

Place the bowl outside in a sunny spot. Lay the hour-hand stick directly in the shadow stick's shadow.

1

Fill a bowl with sand or gravel. Stand your shadow stick in the bowl.

3

Return in an hour.
Has the shadow
moved?

4

Come back each hour to
move the hour-hand stick
into its new shadow.

What do you observe?

Let's see where
the shadow falls!

iCE MELT CHALLENGE

HOW WILL YOU FREE THE TOYS?

GROWN-UP PREP STEPS

Freeze at least four small toys or large beads of equal size in an ice cube tray. Gather a small bowl of salt, a small bowl of baking soda, a cup of warm water, and two plates.

1

Freeze some small toys inside ice cubes.

How will they escape?

The toy is poking out.

2

Put one ice cube
on each of the
two plates.

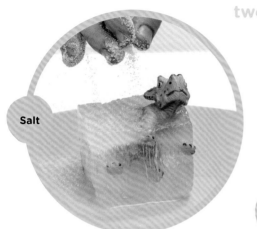

Salt

Baking
Soda

3

Sprinkle salt on one cube, and
sprinkle baking soda on the other.

Oooh,
that's cold!

4

Drop another cube into
the cup of warm water.

5

Pick up one more cube
and hold it in your hand.

Which of the four ice cubes melts and frees the toy fastest?

SOUND SCAVENGER HUNT

WHAT DO YOUR EARS TELL YOU THAT YOUR EYES DON'T?

Chickadee-dee-dee

GROWN-UP PREP STEPS

This listening activity requires no special materials. Extend the activity by helping your child create a sound scavenger hunt for family members or friends to try.

1

Sit somewhere comfortable and close your eyes.

I can hear the wind!

Was that a school bus or helicopter?

2

What sounds do you hear?

Describe any sounds you can't identify.

3

Try listening indoors and outdoors, and at different times of day.

Are the sounds different?

CEREAL STATIC

WHAT WILL MAKE THE CEREAL MOVE?

GROWN-UP PREP STEPS

Tie an O-shaped piece of cereal to a 7- or 8-inch piece of string or thread. Gather a plastic comb and different fabrics, including wool, cotton, and silk.

1

Hold the comb next to the hanging cereal.

What happens?

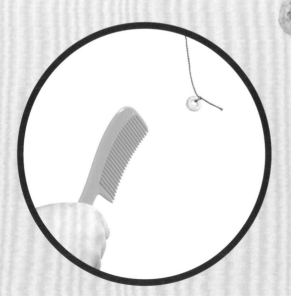

2

Now comb your hair (or a friend's).

It's swinging!

3

Hold the comb next to the cereal again.

Now what happens?

4

Experiment by rubbing the comb against different fabrics and then holding it near the cereal.

WASH THAT WATER!

CAN YOU CLEAN UP DIRTY WATER THE WAY NATURE DOES?

GROWN-UP PREP STEPS

To create this filter, you will need a 2-liter plastic bottle, cheesecloth or a screen, a rubber band, and a clear cup. Help your child collect dirty water from a mud puddle or mix dirt into clean water to pour through the filter. The materials for the inside of the filter should range from coarse (such as gravel or wood chips) to fine (such as sand).

Note: The "clean" water is **not** safe to drink!

1

Have a grown-up help you cut the bottle in half.

Attach a few layers of cheesecloth or a screen over the bottle's mouth with a rubber band.

2

Place the bottle upside-down over a clear cup.

Pour muddy water into the bottle so it flows through the cloth.

Does the water change?

Finer material works best toward the bottom. Experiment!

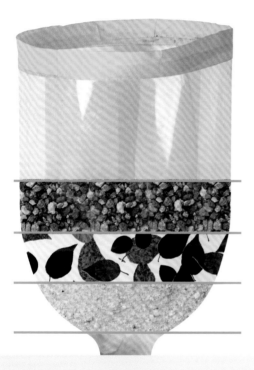

I can see through it now!

3

Collect stuff to put in your bottle to help clean the water.

Try sand, gravel, cotton balls, clean leaves, or wood chips. Layer them inside the bottle.

4

Pour in more dirty water.

Does it take longer to flow through?

How clear can the water get?

Empty your bottle and try different materials.

SHAKE iT UP!

CAN YOU CHANGE A CREAMY LIQUID TO A BUTTERY SOLID?

GROWN-UP PREP STEPS

Gather half a cup of heavy cream and an 8-ounce jar with a secure lid. Remember to let your child taste the whipped cream stage! If you shake long enough, it will turn into a lump of butter.

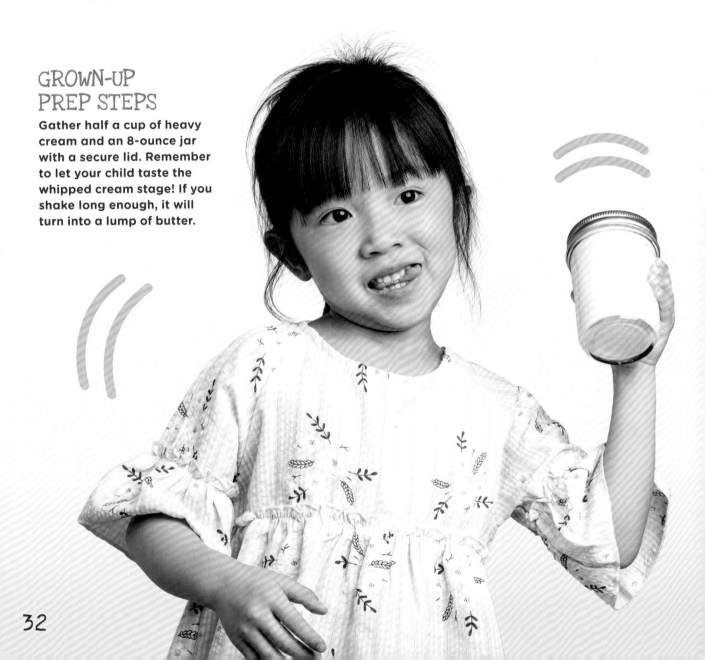

1

Pour the cream into the jar. Screw the lid on tight.

It's getting clumpy!

2

Shake the jar to add energy. Taste the whipped cream!

Want a taste?

3

Keep shaking! How does the cream change? Can you shake it long enough to make butter?

ANIMAL TRACKERS

WHAT STORIES DO ANIMAL TRACKS TELL?

GROWN-UP PREP STEPS

There are two parts to this investigation. First, gather some plastic animal toys with realistic-looking feet. Get out play dough or modeling clay to let your child experiment with making tracks. Second, look for areas where animals have left tracks in mud or snow.

1

Gather up some of your toy animals and look at their feet.

2

Walk your animals across a piece of play dough or modeling clay. What do their tracks look like?

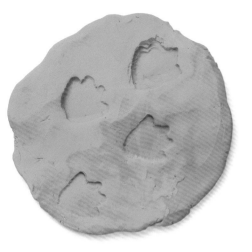

3

Tell a story about each animal and where it is going.

4

Now go outside and look for tracks in the mud or snow. What stories do they tell?

My giraffe is going to find some leaves to eat!

HiDDEN COLORS

WHAT HAPPENS WHEN LIGHT PASSES THROUGH A PRISM?

GROWN-UP PREP STEPS

For this activity, you will need a small prism (sometimes called a "suncatcher") that you can hang in a window. Collect white paper, tape, and colored pencils or crayons in rainbow colors.

1

Hang the prism in a sunny window so that the light shines through it. Look around you.

What do you notice?

2

Find a surface where the prism is making a rainbow. Tape the white paper over the colors.

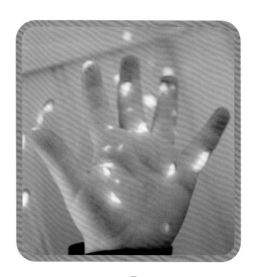

3

Color over the rainbow with crayons or colored pencils that match.

4

Turn the prism or experiment with moving it to another place.

Do the colors stay the same?

CLIMATE PAL

FIND A PEN PAL WHO LIVES FAR AWAY.
IS THE TEMPERATURE DIFFERENT THERE THAN WHERE YOU ARE?

GROWN-UP PREP STEPS

Help your child find a friend or relative who lives in a different climate. Hang an easy-to-read thermometer outside. On a large piece of paper, create a graph with your child, showing the seven days of the week along the x-axis and a range of temperatures along the y-axis. Help your child communicate (text, email, video conference) with their Climate Pal. Extend the activity by finding both locations on a globe or map.

1

Ask someone to be your Climate Pal!

2

What's the weather like today? Check your thermometer.

3

Mark the temperature on your graph.

4

Keep checking and recording the weather at the same time each day for a week. Ask your Climate Pal to do the same.

5

Share and compare your results.

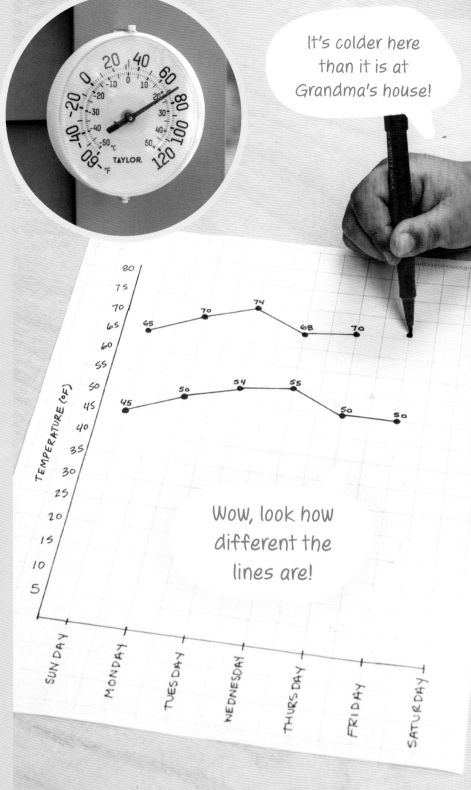

THE NOSE KNOWS

WHAT CAN YOU TELL FROM A SMELL?

Coffee Beans

Cinnamon Sticks

GROWN-UP PREP STEPS

This activity works best with at least three strongly scented foods or spices, such as cinnamon, oregano, cardamom, or coffee beans. Extend the activity by adding more foods. Use a blindfold instead of closing eyes, if you'd like.

1

In your kitchen, look for three or more spices or other foods that have a strong smell. What you smell are gases!

Cardamom Pods

2

Close your eyes and have a grown-up help you smell one food at a time. Can you guess what each one is?

This is strong. A lot of gas must be escaping.

Mmmm, this one is my favorite.

3

Now open your eyes. Did you guess right about what you were smelling? What smelled the strongest?

BACKYARD BIRD COUNT

BE A COMMUNITY SCIENTIST! HOW MANY BIRD COLORS DO YOU SEE?

GROWN-UP PREP STEPS

Help your child fill a backyard bird feeder or find a place where birds visit. Create a tally sheet to count the number of birds of different colors that you see (for example, red, blue, gray, brown, and black birds). Extend the activity by using a bird guide to identify bird species. You can help your child upload their findings to a database app, such as eBird.

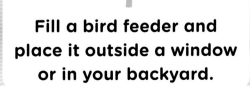

1

Fill a bird feeder and place it outside a window or in your backyard.

42

So many colors!

There's a blue bird now.

2

Sit quietly and wait for a bird to come to the feeder.

3

What color is the bird? Make a tally mark next to the color.

4

Keep observing, using tally marks to count how many birds of each color you see.

43

NOTES FOR BiG PEOPLE

Preschoolers are constantly learning about their environment, using all of their senses to observe and explore. As you do the activities in this book, encourage your young scientist to use vocabulary that corresponds to the scientific ideas they are exploring. Below is a guide to the scientific method and the concepts introduced in each activity.

THE SCIENTIFIC METHOD

Preschoolers instinctively use the steps of the scientific method to explore their world. What is more natural than to ask a question about what you observe—the first step in any scientific research?

Children often ask questions about their everyday lives: *Why does a ball roll down a hill? What is a shadow? Why does a baking cake change shape? How do plants grow?* When they do, you can use the vocabulary of science to further excite their curiosity. Encourage them to guess, or formulate a hypothesis, about what they think will happen or has happened.

The next step is to design an experiment to test their predictions. *Watch what happens* is another way to say *observe and collect data*. There are many ways to help children collect data, or information—from drawing pictures of what they see to keeping tallies or making simple graphs or charts. These visual means of collecting information will help them draw conclusions, the final stage in the scientific method.

Each activity in *Busy Little Hands: Science Play!* involves the steps of the scientific method, starting with a question. Children can engage with the activities at any level. If you wish to reinforce the five steps of the scientific method, here's an example using the first activity, Pulley-Up.

- The activity begins with a **question**: How high can you lift a heavy load?

- Ask children to predict, or form a **hypothesis**, about how much they can lift and how high they can lift their load.

- Then, help them **design an experiment** comparing two methods of lifting. You might hint at using the rope as a pulley or see if they come up with the idea without your help.

- Discuss how they might keep track of their results, or **collect data**. They could list or draw pictures of the collection of objects they can lift using both methods. With your help, they could also use a measuring tape to measure and record how high they lift the load off the ground.

- Finally, talk to children about what they discovered. Can they **draw conclusions**? Are there other questions they want to explore?

Physics

Physics is the study of objects and the forces acting upon them. It describes how objects move and how energy—including light, heat, and electricity—behaves. The activities below introduce children to how these concepts relate to the world around them.

Pulley-Up (pages 4–5) experiments with the concept of **work** by making a simple pulley system. Work is the amount of **force** it takes to move an object over a distance. Force is defined as a push or a pull. A pulley is a simple machine used to redirect force. For example, instead of lifting a load by pulling up, a pulley allows you to pull down, an easier motion.

Polar Bear Paw (pages 12–13) explores the concept of **insulation**. Insulation is any material that stops the flow of heat or cold, sound, or electricity from passing from one substance to another. A layer of fat, called blubber, in polar bears and some other arctic animals, serves as insulation, protecting their bodies from extreme temperatures.

Kitchen Sink or Float (pages 20–21) experiments with **density**. Density is how much space an object takes up relative to how much matter, or "stuff," is in it. Regardless of weight, if an object is more tightly packed with matter, it is more dense. A piece of clay is more dense than water, so it sinks. Wax is less dense than water, so a wax candle floats.

Cereal Static (pages 28–29) experiments with **static electricity**, the buildup of electrical charge on an object's surface. Static electricity is produced when two objects touch one another and electrons (very small pieces of matter and energy) move from one object to the other. For example, when you comb your hair, electrons move from your hair to the comb, causing the electrical charges to change.

Hidden Colors (pages 36–37) is an investigation of **light**. White light, such as ordinary daylight, is composed of all the visible colors—red, orange, yellow, green, blue, and violet. When daylight passes through a prism, the prism's facets separate it into the visible colors.

Earth Science

Earth science is the study of the planet Earth, including its lands and waters and the air surrounding it. The activities below invite children to explore such earth science concepts as precipitation and the water cycle, climate, geologic forces, and Earth's rotation.

Vinegar Volcano (pages 6–7) uses a simple chemical reaction to demonstrate the **pressure** that causes a volcanic eruption. Pressure is the amount of force acting on an area. Pressure is important in forming rock, including igneous, or volcanic, rock. High pressure leads to the creation of magma (melted rock). Volcanoes erupt because magma beneath the surface is less dense than rock above it, creating upward pressure. Over time, this pressure builds up, and magma pushes to the surface.

Rain, Rain, Come to Stay (pages 14–15) is about collecting and measuring **precipitation**. Precipitation can take the form of rain, mist, snow, sleet, or hail. It is part of the water cycle, the path that water takes as it moves around the earth in different states. This activity can also be used to introduce the concept of conservation, the process of protecting things in nature. When people take care in their everyday lives to use only what they need, or to recycle or safely reuse things (such as water), they are practicing conservation.

Shadow Clock (pages 22–23) explores the movement of **shadows** due to the rotation of the earth. A shadow is a dark area produced when an object comes between a light source and a surface. Shadows of stationary objects move and change shape because the earth rotates, changing the position of objects relative to the sun.

Wash That Water! (pages 30–31) is about creating a simple **filtration** system. Filtration is the process of removing dirt or other solids from liquid. Nature filters water through wetlands, the rushing of streams over rocks, the seeping of water into soil, and other methods. Drinking water must go through a filtration system using advanced technologies.

Climate Pal (pages 38–39) is an exploration of **climate** and **weather**. Climate is the average temperature and the combination of winds, air moisture, and snow and rain in a particular area over many years. Climate conveys a larger picture than weather, which is what happens in a single day.

Chemistry

Chemistry is the study of matter, or what things are made of, and how energy changes matter. Matter is any substance that takes up space and can exist as a solid, liquid, or gas. The chemistry activities below allow children to explore different forms of matter in their world and experience firsthand how matter changes with the addition of energy.

Blooming Colors (pages 8–9) is an experiment with simple **chromatography**. Chromatography is a method of separating mixtures and can be used to separate color mixtures into their pure pigments. For example, orange ink can be separated into yellow and red. Black inks are a mixture of several pigments.

Mystery Goop (pages 16–17) is a substance you can make that sometimes acts like a **solid** and sometimes acts like a **liquid**. Solid and liquid are two of the three states of matter (the third is gas). Something in a solid state keeps the same shape, unless the temperature or pressure changes. A wood block is a solid, as are books, clothes, and furniture. Liquid is the state of matter between solid and gas. Liquid can be thought of as taking the shape of whatever contains it, the way water or juice takes the shape of a pitcher or glass.

Ice Melt Challenge (pages 24–25) explores how water changes from a solid phase (ice) to a liquid. **Phase change** is the transformation of matter from one state, or condition, to another. Changing temperature and pressure can cause material to change states from solid to liquid to gas and back again.

Shake It Up! (pages 32–33) is a way for children to use their own **energy** to change matter from liquid to solid. Energy is the power it takes to make things move or change. Energy can come in the form of heat, electricity, or work. To produce butter, children apply their energy through the work of shaking heavy cream.

The Nose Knows (pages 40–41) explores the **gas** phase of matter. Gas is the state of matter that has no fixed shape or volume and can expand indefinitely. The air we breathe is composed of gases. Odors are gases as well.

Biology

Biology is the study of living things. The activities below introduce biology concepts as they relate to a child's outdoor environment. These field-based activities also offer a window into the role of scientists in making and sharing unique discoveries.

Seed Start (pages 10–11) explores the question of what is needed for **life**. Life is characterized by the ability to use energy to grow, respond to changes in the environment, and reproduce. Living things need air, water, and food.

Biodiversity Hoop (pages 18–19) introduces the concept of **biodiversity**, the great variety of life on Earth. The richness of plants, animals, bacteria, fungi, and other life-forms is not only a source of wonder and fascination but is also essential to the health of our planet's ecosystems.

Sound Scavenger Hunt (pages 26–27) explores the **sense** of hearing. Our senses allow us to gather information about the world. Humans have five senses: sight, smell, hearing, touch, and taste.

Animal Trackers (pages 34–35) is an investigation of **animal signs**. Animal signs are imprints (tracks) or other evidence—such as a hole, a gnawed plant, or scat (poop)—that show where an animal has been. Signs can be used to identify animals and learn about their movements and actions.

Backyard Bird Count (pages 42–43) is an introduction to **community science**. Community science is the idea that everyone can contribute to scientific discoveries by observing their own environments. Children can learn they are never too young to observe and share what they find in their communities.

YOUR SCIENCE FIELD KIT

Every good scientist needs a field kit! This handy tool kit contains just a few of the things you might use to observe and record your scientific findings. Feel free to fill your field kit with what you like and need for your own explorations. Store these items in a small backpack or field bag, and keep it handy for your next adventure!

Field guides (or online app such as iNaturalist)

Compass

Binoculars

Magnet

Notebook

Crayons, pastels, or markers

Tape measure

1m–3ft

Magnifying lens

Prism

Small containers for collecting specimens

Thermometer

String or twine

Pencil or fine-tipped pen

The mission of Storey Publishing is to serve our customers by publishing practical information that encourages personal independence in harmony with the environment.

Edited by Deanna F. Cook and Hannah Fries
Art direction and book design by Ash Austin
Text production by Ian O'Neill

Cover photography by Mars Vilaubi © Storey Publishing, LLC except © Alexstart/stock.adobe.com, front (ladybugs); © Carlos Santa Maria/stock.adobe .com, front (butterfly); Mehdi Sepehri/Unsplash, back (birds); © uwimages/stock.adobe.com, front (seedlings)
Interior photography by Mars Vilaubi © Storey Publishing, LLC
Additional photography by © Cara Brstrom/Stocksy, 36 (prism); © freeject.net/stock.adobe.com, 36 (background); © jamie grill atlas/Stocksy, 37 (#4); Johnny Such/Unsplash, 26 (sky); © luckybusiness/ stock.adobe.com, 23 (children); © meoita/stock .adobe.com, 27 (helicopter); © Mikhailov Studio/ stock.adobe.com, 18 (grass); © RyersonClark/ iStock.com, 35 (snowy tracks); © Stuart Monk/ stock.adobe.com, 27 (school bus); © Yann Wirthor/ stock.adobe.com, 27 (pinwheel)
Props by Ann Lewis
Illustrations by © Jannie Ho, except endpapers, 2–3 (background), 4–5 (grass) by Ash Austin © Storey Publishing, LLC

Text © 2022 by Susan Edwards Richmond

Storey books are available at special discounts when purchased in bulk for premiums and sales promotions as well as for fund-raising or educational use. Special editions or book excerpts can also be created to specification. For details, please call 800-827-8673, or send an email to sales@storey.com.

Storey Publishing
210 MASS MoCA Way
North Adams, MA 01247
storey.com

Printed in China by Shenzhen Reliance Printing Co. Ltd.
10   9   8   7   6   5   4   3   2   1

Library of Congress Cataloging-in-Publication Data on file